GHOST ENCOUNTERS

13 True Tales of the Supernatural

Shanna Warner

ISBN: 978-1-953098-00-9

Published by: Manna Services Group, LLC
Tulsa, OK - September 2020

Note: These stories are all true, but some names, dates, locations, and certain details not pertinent to the main action have been changed to protect the identities of those who shared them with me.

This book is dedicated to my three favorite men:
Mark, Joshua, and Matthew.
I love sitting around with you guys talking of things
that go bump in the night. And a special dedication
for David, who indeed went bump.

And also to you, dear reader!
Make a drink, grab a snack, and enjoy.

CONTENTS

INTRODUCTION

"There are more things in Heaven and Earth, Horatio, than are dreamt of in your philosophy."- Shakespeare's Hamlet

DO YOU BELIEVE IN GHOSTS? Start listening to the people around you and subtle hints of stories just like the ones in this book will show up. Your first inclination might be to discount those stories, because to the rational mind they sound irrational. It just sounds too weird.

The idea of ghosts and hauntings did not make sense to me for a long time. Over the years with each new story and experience my perspective has changed. I have become a believer! (Mostly.) I do not believe everything I read or hear – only a fool does. What I do believe is this: some things exist beyond the accepted knowledge of what we consider "reality." What are ghosts, spirits, angels, and demons? I have no idea. Do people have life-changing experiences with these unknown entities? Yes, they do.

I have had weird experiences throughout my life, beginning in childhood. But I have always used my rational, scientific mind to try to understand and categorize the experiences as something entirely rational and understandable. That was part of the problem. We just cannot really look at ghosts with our rational minds; we must hear and experience these stories with our emotional, spiritual minds.

That does not mean that you must go all "woo-woo" crazy and ignore your rational, scientific mind in order to "believe" in ghosts. No, it just means you must admit that science does not have all the answers. You can admit that, right?

Just a few hundred years ago, science told us the Earth was flat, and bloodletting was the answer to illness. Doctors once told us that mental illness could be cured by pounding a hole in someone's skull to let the demons out. See, science is a work in progress. We learn more with each discovery. I believe that will happen with the phenomenon of ghosts. Eventually, science will be able to explain to us just what really does happen to the soul after death. Or what the soul really is.

It all started for me as a child with Granny telling me stories that she did not share with many people. But the final experience that cemented my belief in ghosts occurred just a few years back when my deceased husband came to check on me one night. I thought it was my NEW hubby coming to bed, but no. (You can read that story in the last chapter.)

My Granny is the reason I became fascinated with ghosts at an early age. She and I would tell each other stories. The difference was that HER stories were true. She did not tell the ladies at Sunday church school about the demon visitor, but she told me. I miss my Granny! (And no, she has never visited me as a ghost, although she has brought messages in my dreams.) Her daughter, my mom, loves to read. When mom discovered I had a craving for ghost stories, she kept my little library well-stocked. No one else in my family, except my Granny, was fascinated with the supernatural.

I was a little girl back in the 70s, and every Friday night I would watch this television series called "The Nightstalker." Each week, the hero of the series battled demons, vampires, witches or ghosts. I watched it all alone because everyone else in my family thought it was too weird and scary. I know Granny would have watched it with me, but she lived in town and did not know how to drive.

In this book you will hear true stories of child ghosts, animal ghosts, visions, demonic visitors, life-saving ghosts, angel hugs, and some truly weird phenomena. ALL of these stories are true. Each story either happened to me or some brave soul told me all about their spooky experience.

Some of the situations in this book have been slightly changed, and names have been altered. This is to protect personal information and identities of those who shared these stories.

So, settle in and get ready for some fun. Go grab something to drink or snack on and get comfortable. But just a gentle warning to you:

do not read this book on a dark and stormy night, unless all the lights are on.

Enjoy my true ghost stories!

LITTLE PEOPLE AT THE DOOR

They might look cute, but looks can definitely be deceiving.

LEA WAS MY COUSIN BY MARRIAGE. We like to joke that I got her and her daughter Michelle in the divorce decree. They have been a part of my life now for decades since I divorced their cousin.

Before our son was born, my husband and I moved to the big city where I got to know these two lovely ladies and their extended family.

I had always been interested in ghosts, and Lea had a couple of what we called "hot spots" at her house. This was before I really knew how to investigate (and get rid of) ghosts. Thankfully, I knew enough to keep us safe.

Whatever ghosts are, some seem harmless, and more to be pitied because they cannot cross over to wherever ghosts go when they no longer have a body. But some of them are quite unpleasant. There have been reports of ghosts doing physical harm to people. That harm seems to come from a place of hate and rage. Not all ghosts are like the friendly ghosts from popular childhood books and cartoons.

The ghosts at Lea's house were sneaky. They seemed harmless at first. They were just a couple of cute little kid ghosts who wanted to come in and play. But I believe they were dangerous. I believe they wanted Lea and Michelle to think they were harmless so they would open the door and let them in. That is why they took the appearance of little children.

There was a shed in Lea's backyard that was scary beyond the typical dark and gloomy shed. If you can imagine a shed having a bad attitude, well, this one was just grumpy. It seemed to be waiting to trip you up with a piece of plywood or a rusty nail that just shows up in your pathway. We did not enter the shed unless it was necessary because it seemed so negative.

Not only did the shed seem to have bad vibes, it also made weird noises. Several times, there seemed to be a whistling sound coming from inside the shed. Oklahoma is known for being a state where "the wind comes sweeping down the plains." But the whistling sound would happen even when there was no wind. You would step outside the door and the sound would stop. Step inside the door and the sound started up again. Weird.

The shed seemed to be the main hotspot outside the home. And that is possibly where the children came from. Two little kids would show up at the front door of the house. They never spoke, but would just wave and act like they wanted to come in.

The first time they showed up, Lea and Michelle thought they were real. They looked once and the children were there, looked again and the children were gone. The ladies walked outside thinking that maybe they were neighborhood children who were just stopping by to say hello. But after that first sighting, the ladies looked closer and saw that the "children" seemed to be slightly transparent. Well, that was unusual for sure.

Lea and Michelle got accustomed to seeing the children at the door. They even talked about the possibility of opening the door and inviting them in. But something, some inner sense that the situation was not quite right, kept them from opening the door.

"NO! Do not open the door," that was my answer when the ladies asked me. "Listen, you guys already have that gut feeling that says no. Well, listen to your instincts! Do NOT open the door."

I think opening the door could have led to some negative consequences for them. When you actually allow or even invite forces into your home, then be prepared for all hell to break loose. Or be prepared to manage as best you can. OR just do not invite unknown forces into your home. There, that is just about the best advice I can ever give. Trust those instincts! If it feels wrong and dangerous, then it probably is.

Even without letting ghost children come in, there was already weirdness going on in the house. A foggy, wisp of a cloud would show up and float around the ceiling in the kitchen and living room. I saw it several times. The family had become accustomed to seeing the fog, and never could find a reason for it. The first time I saw it, I thought it was steam – like when you lift the lid from a pot of boiling spaghetti. But no one was cooking.

Another strange situation was with their dog, a great big Chow. He had a special hatred reserved just for me. He would come over and sit in front of me and growl. He would even sometimes put his chin on my knee and just slobber like a maniac. He really hated me! He loved everyone else. Maybe he thought I was bringing the weirdness?

Once they eventually moved out of that house, he and I became great friends. He was happy to see me. He was a different dog around me. I was the only person he ever hated, but only while in that house.

There was one last strange happening in the home that I got to experience. Michelle was still a teenager living at home. My husband and I were visiting. He and Michelle were laughing about that one little weird doll she had. Her bedroom seemed to be a place where dolls and toys would come to life, even when the batteries were removed. Once the laughter died down, we could hear a muffled-sounding voice. It was high-pitched like a child's toy and it was coming from Michelle's room.

We all ran into the room while she began digging through the piles of toys that were cluttering the back of her closet. She could not even remember the last time she saw the doll. She had kept it just because it had been her favorite as a child. Sure enough, the talking doll was there at the bottom of the pile. We could hear it and see it talk. And it had no batteries. It did not speak any discernible words or phrases, but mainly made noises that sounded more like muffled conversation.

That was one of the creepiest moments for me. I asked them why they kept it. Both decided that keeping a creepy doll was not a good thing, and since they could not come up with a reason for it to stay in the home, they decided to get rid of it. But instead of putting the doll in the trash, we decided that the children in the shed could have the doll.

That night, as we left, I reminded them that they were to never open the door to the children, no matter how cute they looked. They agreed. They also agreed to take the doll to the shed, where it stayed for the remainder of the time they lived in the house.

Moving the doll to the shed seemed to pacify the children, because they were seen less frequently. Eventually, Lea and Michelle moved out of that house. At first, they were afraid the activity would follow them to a new home. Thankfully, it did not. I think those particular ghosts were attached to that house and remained behind.

That was nearly thirty years ago. Neither of them has seen or heard anything quite so terrifying as those ghostly children who probably were not children at all.

THE THING IN THE CLOSET

"Don't worry, he never comes out."

I WAS DATING A NICE YOUNG MAN. We were headed to visit with his family. On the way, he warned me about some "thing" that lived in the closet of his childhood bedroom at his Mom's house. I thought he was just teasing; he and I loved to tell each other weird and crazy stories.

His mom and dad, along with a teenage sister and a brother, were still living in the home. After dinner, I mentioned the story that he told me. I expected smiles and laughter. Instead, I got frightened looks and warnings. I quickly learned that everyone else in his family was afraid to spend the night in that bedroom. It had become the "guest" room.

It turns out that he had grown up in a profoundly dysfunctional household. His mom had been neglectful and abusive to him and his siblings. He had also grown up in a narrow-minded religion where the church met in a building with no windows. This was supposedly for privacy from non-believers, but it also allowed privacy for the leaders to abuse many of the children.

It is understandable to me now that he was an emotionally fragile child. All of his siblings were abused children, too. This may be part of the reason for the "thing" in the closet. Was it a projection? Was it a poltergeist? Neither of us have any answers.

As a child, he did not have control over the adults that were abusing him. His home life was miserable, and he wanted to escape. As he got older, in his pre-teen and early teen years, he would sneak out of his bedroom window to meet up with friends. They were not hooligans; they did not go around spray-painting buildings or breaking into cars. But they did dabble with some spiritual forces.

At some point, he created a ritual and asked for spirits to come and "fix" the situation at home. He wanted to protect his younger siblings and he wanted to be removed from the emotional, psychological, and physical abuse. Or as an alternative, he wanted his mother removed from the home.

During one of the rituals, he got an answer. It was in the form of an "energy creature" that followed him home and lived in his closet. It was not visible, but at least once it spoke to him. He got a protective spirit that kept everyone else out of his bedroom!

I know – it sounds too weird to be true. I did not really believe him at first, but I got to witness the phenomena first-hand. No one in the family could see it, but they heard it in the closet. It was capable of moving objects and making noise.

At first, the family had used the room for storage. But just walking into the room made them feel uncomfortable. Since no one would sleep in the room, they tried to use the closet as storage. No one wanted to leave their clothes in that closet. Imagine putting on a shirt only to find that something else was in it, too. Eventually, they moved everything out. All that was left behind were some extra hangers, and the basic furnishings for a guest room.

Family members reported to me that the hangers would clack and clank around at night. It sounded like something was playing with them, making them hit each other. If you scooted all the hangers to one side, by morning they would be spread out over the closet rod.

The parents had tried removing the hangers, but the noises continued. Without the hangers, the noises sounded more like scratching sounds in the walls of the closet.

The family decided that the noise of hangers clanking around was preferable to the noise of scratching. As long as whatever it was stayed in that room and that closet, then it could play with the hangers all it wanted!

As we went to bed that night, my boyfriend explained more about how he would sneak out when he lived there and how he asked spirits to come and remove the negative influences at his home. That was not quite the bedtime story I was hoping for. It was unsettling to think of abuse and childhood fantasies of retribution and revenge. I was not sure if I would be able to sleep at all.

Once he realized just how upset I was, he explained that the energy creature had never once harmed anyone. He believed it was a protective spirit that would keep anyone safe in the room. That made me feel a bit better. He even offered to speak to it if it got too noisy during the night. He took the time to open the closet door and tell the thing to mind its manners and be quiet for the night.

I joined him at the closet door. It was small. And looked normal. It had one rod to hang clothes on and one shelf above that. There was nothing in the closet except about 10-12 hangers shoved all the way to the right side.

"See, there's nothing to be afraid of. It listens to me," he said. He hopped into bed and quickly fell asleep.

I got into bed, too, and just hoped for a good night's sleep. But the closet thing did not listen to the instructions. Instead, the noise woke me up in the middle of the night. I had not been sleeping well anyway, with strange dreams circling around in my head. As soon as I woke up, I knew what was going on.

My boyfriend was sleeping deeply. I did not want to disturb him, so I lay there for a while listening to his snores. The sounds in the closet were just as annoying. It was just clickety-clack, clickety-clack, back and forth. I poked my boyfriend to make him stop snoring while trying to decide if I should get out of bed.

The curiosity was just too much for me to resist. I turned on the bedside lamp and slowly sat up. I wanted to "catch" the activity as it was happening, so I quietly walked to the closet door. I could still hear the noises. I opened the door as slowly as possible. I saw the hangers swinging, now in the middle of the closet, as if someone had just been playing with them. And I guess that someone or some "thing" had.

The next morning, after breakfast, I thanked my hostess and her family. No one asked how I slept, or if I had heard the closet noises. Maybe they did not want to know.

As we left that home, I vowed to never sleep in the room again. It was not because of the protective spirit. It was because the man I was sitting beside had needed the protection from his mother and other abusive adults. That was far more terrifying.

HER BROTHER CAME TO SAY GOODBYE

Because Family is Forever.

MY GRANNY WAS FULL OF GREAT STORIES. She thought it was cute that I would make up stories about "my cousins" who could do all sorts of fabulous things. As a child, I had dreams about creatures that could fly and could climb tall buildings. I called them "cousins." The stories I told her came from those dreams and visions I had, and from my Irish imagination, too.

I would tell her those stories and she would tell me stories about the "Little People." Eventually, she started telling me stories about ghosts and other spirits. They were happy little stories, until one day, she told me of something that was not quite so happy.

My granny was Irish. She had been born in America, but her heart was in the Emerald Isle. When she told me about "Little People" I always thought of them like the creatures from my dreams. They were small, but could do mighty things. I thought they were wonderful, because they lived inside caves or under the roots of trees along a riverbank.

They were mischievous and usually up to no good. If you met one, well, you had best keep your wits about you and never turn your back on it. You could be pretty sure one was nearby if you were out in nature, and the hairs on the back of your neck or arms started to stand up, even if it was broad daylight. And do not ever let it follow you home!

It was not wise to go looking for them, she said. But of course, like any country kid, I was always turning over rocks and looking in holes. I was looking for crawdads or worms or snakes, but if I found the hidden home of the little people, well that was even better.

She loved to tell me those stories, and I knew it was all in good fun. But there came a day when Granny started telling me stories that were not kind and gentle. As I got older, the stories she shared with me got to the very heart of our belief systems about religion and life after death. I knew those stories were different. They were frightening because they were real.

My Granny was a devout Christian. She attended church and knew the literature of the Bible like she knew the stories from the old country. She would routinely read a passage from the Bible every morning and every evening. So, she knew the creatures from the holy writings as well as she knew the creatures from Irish literature.

(She once told me that angels would protect me from the man behind the door. I had no idea at the time what she was talking about, but later in life, that came true. Although that is another story for another book.)

When the day came that she told me about the demon showing up in her house, I believed her. She was asleep when this unknown creature visited. The smell is what woke her. It was nasty, like burning trash. At first, she thought her house was on fire.

It took her a moment to grab her glasses and switch on the lamp. The hairs on her arms and the back of her neck were standing up, so she knew something was very wrong.

That is when she saw the creature. It was grey and wrinkled. It was a bit smaller than a human adult, and the face was more like a cross between a wolf and a bat. It did not speak and did not attempt to touch her. It just stood in the doorway of her closet and stared at her.

Of course, she was frightened, but like a good Irish lass, she kept her wits about her.

She always kept a high-powered pellet gun beside her bed, and considered using it on the creature. But she recognized it as a spiritual force, not as a purely physical manifestation. She knew that the spiritual problem would need a spiritual solution.

As she became fully awake and aware, she was actually more angry than afraid. When she told me about the creature, I was terrified. But she explained to me that as children of the Divine Spirit, we can claim power over negative forces. And how dare some negative force come bother her anyway?

She grabbed her Bible, and told the creature to leave her home! She demanded that it leave.

And it did. In an instant, in the blink of an eye, the creature was gone. It never returned.

She told me this, not as allegory or parable, but as truth. I knew my Granny to be an honest person. I knew when she was telling funny stories and I knew when she was being serious. The story about the demon was true, just like the story about her brother, my great-uncle Hezzekiah.

Uncle Hezzie seemed nice enough, just quieter and more introspective than his sister. My Granny was light-hearted and always ready for a smile and a laugh. Uncle Hezzie seemed far more serious than his little sister. He did not smile much and did not seem too fond of noisy little children, especially curious little ones like me who told big stories.

His visit with Granny was only for a few days. He was in poor health and was headed to the veteran's center to see a doctor. The next time we went to Granny's house, she said that Hezzie had come to see her again but that it was his last visit.

During the day, Granny usually left her heavy, front door open with just the screen door locked. She loved the breeze and being able to hear nature sounds. She could also hear when someone walked up onto her porch or pulled into the gravel driveway.

She was in the kitchen at the back of the house when she heard someone at the front door. She popped her head around the door to take a peek. It was Hezzie! She waved at him, and he waved right back and smiled. At that moment, the phone rang. She turned around to grab it and looked back at the front door. But Hezzie was gone!

She lifted the phone up to her ear and said hello. As she listened to the voice on the line, it was the veteran's hospital. They had called to inform her, Hezzekiah McBride's next of kin, that he had just passed away. But she already knew. He had not been waving hello. He had been waving good-bye!

THIS IS NOT YOUR HOUSE

A midnight snack for Angie.

MOST REALTORS ARE GREAT AT FINDING THE PERFECT HOUSE FOR YOUR FAMILY. And usually, the old occupants leave the house long before the new occupants move in. Usually. My realtor friend told me this story about a home she sold and the family that got far more than just a beautiful place to live.

The house was gorgeous. The family could not believe they could afford the stately mansion. Once known as the "Oil Capital of the World," Tulsa has some fabulous homes that were built in the oil heyday of the 20s and 30s. They just did not come on the market very often. The realtor knew the home was a historical treasure and a bargain. It was a 2-story home with plenty of room for a big family. She had the perfect family in mind; they had four boys and three dogs.

The dad had been transferred to Tulsa from Fort Worth, and they hoped the transfer would be permanent. The mom, Angie, loved their new home and wanted to dive into a remodeling project. The wallpaper in the kitchen and bathrooms had to go. It was just too old-fashioned. Thankfully, the home had great structure and was built to last. All the remodeling would mostly be cosmetic!

Like in most homes, the kitchen was their family hub. They spent a lot of time there - cooking, talking and just being together. It had a good flow, and a good feel to it, and the prior homeowner had modernized all the appliances. Keeping all her kids and pets fed meant that the kitchen was always in use, so she was glad it needed nothing but a touchup of paint.

Every morning, Angie was the first to rise. She would head downstairs to start the coffee maker. She loved her kitchen, it was bright and cheery, and the perfect place for coffee with her hubby before the kids got up. Every morning she would find at least one kitchen door or drawer open. She and her husband started checking the kitchen at night together. Both would verify that cabinet doors and drawers were all closed. And every morning, a drawer or door in the kitchen would be open. Sometimes two.

The likely culprit? Their rambunctious boys. They checked on them often at night to see if one of them was sleep-walking to go sleep-snacking in the kitchen. Nope. They even had a pest control company come out to check for mice. Nope. They could not figure out what was causing the activity in the kitchen. They always figured they would catch one of the boys in the act someday.

There was a front, formal staircase that led to the four bedrooms and a playroom on the second floor. There was also a back staircase at the end of the upper floor that led directly into the kitchen. A century ago, that staircase would have been for the servants. The master bedroom suite was at the front of the house. The kids' rooms were at the back of the house by the back staircase. The boys loved having quick access to snacks in the kitchen.

Since Angie's husband travelled often for business, she was home alone many times overnight with the boys and the dogs. She felt safe. At first. Then she started noticing the noises in the house. It often sounded like someone was walking down the hallway and down the stairs. Occasionally, the sounds would wake her up at night. When she talked with her husband about the noises, he reminded her that the house was old and old houses are notorious for being creaky.

Even with that explanation, she was still on edge when he was gone. She could not rest and would toss and turn all night. A few times, when the noises woke her, she would peek out into the hallway, but no one was there. The only thing that gave her some peace of mind was their alarm system. A company monitored it, and she also had access to a panel where she could see every window and door. She always verified that the alarm was on and the doors and windows were closed. And yet, the noises continued.

One night when the noises woke her up again, she had a plan of action. She clearly heard someone walking down the back staircase. She would usually just check the monitor, verify that everything was okay, and just go back to sleep. But this time, she decided to finally catch one of the boys in an act of mischief. Would it be the oldest one? He was often the instigator. But that youngest was always looking around for snacks. And the two middle boys were quiet and sneaky, too. She quickly checked the monitors first to make sure it was not a burglar. Everything was secure.

She heard the noises in the kitchen. Surely, one of the boys was trying to sneak another cookie. She grabbed her flashlight and sat down in the dark at the top of the stairs, just waiting to catch a naughty boy sneaking back up after his snack! It was exciting. She had never done this before.

She sat there for a few minutes as her eyes and ears adjusted to the dark. Then she noticed the noises had stopped in the kitchen. She looked down the hallway to the front stairs, but no one was coming up that way. She walked halfway down both staircases, not wanting to miss out on finally catching one of the boys.

Trying to figure out which naughty boy was up and wandering around the house, she took a quick peek into the bedrooms. ALL of the boys were asleep in bed! Then who had walked down the stairs and into the kitchen? Who had been making those noises? And were they going to walk back UP the stairs?!

She decided right then there was no way she was walking into her kitchen in the middle of the night. Since there was no way she was going back to sleep either, she stayed up and checked the cameras throughout the night. There were no more noises in the kitchen, but she thought she heard the television in the family room come on just for a moment and then go back off.

That next morning, she called the security company and had them come out to check the system over. She even upgraded their coverage and had more monitors installed. And yet, the noises continued. It was the same pattern: someone walking down the back stairs, noises in the kitchen, and the odd occasion that she heard either music or the television in the middle of the night.

Her husband never heard anything. And her dogs never heard it either. Everyone else loved the house. Angie was secretly relieved when her husband got a promotion because it meant they could leave the house. They were moving to another state. She and the boys would continue to live in the house while her husband got settled into his new position. He would live in a hotel during the week and come home on the weekends until they could put their house on the market and start all over again in another new home.

She called my realtor friend that sold them the house so they could start the process and put the home back up on the market. Angie casually mentioned the strange noises, the footsteps on the stairs, the sounds of music, and the months of bad sleep.

The realtor was shocked and said, "Oh my, honey, I wish you had told me before now. Sounds like your house is haunted. The original owner of the house died there many years ago. I always wondered if remodeling her house would make her upset. It sounds like you might have a residual haunting."

The realtor also had a home-cleansing business on the side. Not home-cleaning, she did not do blinds. She removed unwanted entities like ghosts. Deceased prior owners or occupants can often haunt their old home, especially if they die in the home or lived there for many years before death.

The little ghost lady did not want to leave her home. She was confused, and just wanted to be in her kitchen. She had to be convinced to move on, to go towards the light and on to wherever it was that she belonged. It took two cleansing sessions before the ghost finally left.

The last few months in that home were quiet and peaceful. There were no more restless nights for Angie. Her kitchen was hers alone! They had one last summer in the home and enjoyed every moment. It had truly become a dream home for all nine of them.

Eventually, the house was sold to another lucky family. They got a beautifully remodeled home, with zero former occupants!

BALLS OF LIGHT

"So, you saw them, too?"

WHEN WE MOVED BACK TO RURAL OKLAHOMA, MY DAD VOWED TO BUILD OUR FAMIY A NEW HOME. And he did. It was a beautiful brick home and did not look spooky from the outside. But inside, there were some truly spooky things that happened there. (This is the first story from that house, and I will save my favorite story about the house for later.)

Dad was very frugal with purchases and used recycled materials when he could. The bricks for the house came from an old building that was scheduled for demolition. He got them for a great deal, but it is possible we got more than just bricks. It is too bad that no one can investigate the home since it burned to the ground several years ago.

Some paranormal investigators believe that energy, entities, or even emotions can attach to inanimate objects. Could the bricks have been "contaminated" with the energy from their original usage? There have been reports of materials, especially those made from natural stones and earth minerals, being conduits for ghostly or paranormal happenings. I do not know much about that, but it is an interesting idea.

The materials could have had something to do with the strange happenings in the house, but the location might have had more to do with it, instead. The house was built near some ancient historical sites, near old Native American villages, and some unmarked graves that had been on a stagecoach route. Maybe that was the energy behind the weird experiences I had there.

Just over in the next pasture from where our house stood, there were several unmarked gravestones. They were clustered under an ancient oak tree, and my dad was pretty sure they had been there for over a century. He had grown up in that same valley, and his family (and my mother's family) had been in that area since before Oklahoma was even a state.

Just to the north of us, there was an ancient Native American village site that was in ruins. It was on private land, but since I knew the owners, I could get permission to visit the site and see the grinding stones and other historical artifacts. After I grew up and left that area, someone destroyed that ancient site. What a tragedy.

To the south of us, there was a graveyard that had been on the Butterfield Stagecoach route. The graveyard was called Mountain Station. I will tell you a great story about that site as a bonus at the end of the book.

Our house was in the valley between all these ancient and mystical sites. And it was made out of recycled materials. It was just the right setup for ghostly happenings - like the night that I first saw the balls of light.

I have always loved to read. As a child, you know that I loved ghost stories, but I also read every science fiction and fantasy book in both the school and the public libraries I had access to. There is nothing better than getting lost in a great book, unless it is getting lost in a great book late at night under the covers with a flashlight when you are supposed to be asleep and not reading! I did that quite often as a kid.

I have needed glasses since I was a little girl in the third grade. It is genetics, probably made worse because of all that reading. When I take off my glasses, then the whole world is blurry to me. It is a really neat effect at the end of the year holidays, which for us was Christmas. The lights on the tree look like soft glowing balls to every near-sighted kiddo like me.

This particular night I was in bed and had just finished a great book. I turned off the flashlight and leaned over to put my glasses on the bedside table. As I turned back around, I noticed a flicker of light. In the closet. Well that was weird. Maybe a lightning bug?

I settled down and was nearly asleep. Then, I heard a slight noise. I sat up in bed, and saw movement. The door to the closet was slowly opening. I was not about to turn over and grab my glasses; I did not want to take my eyes off what was happening! Although I was not sure what WAS happening.

The closet door was fully open, and I saw more than one light in there. The orbs of light were in several colors, all pastel, nothing bright or too colorful. They seemed to pulse slightly. They also seemed to be floating. Each one moved independently of the others.

They were coming OUT of the closet and towards me. Okay, now that made me a bit concerned. But still there was no fear. It was not scary. It was amazing and pretty. I just watched them slowly come out of the closet and gently swirl around. They had been hovering about twelve to eighteen inches off the floor, but they started rising as they headed towards my bed.

Yep, I was about to have an encounter! They came up over my bed and swirled around me. I lay down and just watched as the group of orbs, seven or eight of them, gently swirled and pulsed above my body.

I was really sleepy, it was very late, and I kept drifting off. Each time I opened my eyes, they were still there. No, I did not try to touch them. I do not know why I did not try to touch them. I just remember being sleepy and feeling very relaxed. They did not seem to mean me any harm, so I went to sleep.

Several months later I saw them again. The circumstances that second time were completely different. After that first time I thought it might have been just a dream or I had imagined the whole experience. (You know, because of all those crazy sci-fi books!)

But the second time I saw the glowing orbs I was wide awake. It was right at dusk. I was sitting at the bar between the living room and the kitchen, just reading a book and waiting for everyone else to get home.

From that vantage point I could see to my right all the way down the hallway to the doors for each bedroom. And once again, a sparkle caught my eye. The glowing orbs looked smaller this time because I had my glasses on! And I could see more details as they got closer.

The first time I would have said they were about the size of a cantaloupe. That is because of my poor vision. This time I could see that they were much smaller. They were more like the size of a baseball. They had a darker, more compact center, with the glow pulsing out from there.

This time there were only three or four of them. They paid me no attention whatever. They gently floated down the hallway all the way past the bar where I was sitting and out into the family room. When I got up to look for them in the family room, they had vanished.

I never saw them again. I thought that was the end of the story. I was wrong. I have a little brother. He is twelve years younger than I am. I was in college when he was in first grade! We have always been close. And I was delighted to find out that he had an orb story, too.

One morning, when he was about seven years old, he told our Mom and Dad that he had met the Holy Spirit during the night. Well, my brother has always been a talker and tells great stories, too. My parents often ignored the chatter and all the tall tales he told them.

It turns out that balls of light had come out of that same closet and hovered over him while he was in bed, too. He was not scared. He thought it was a spiritual experience. In his child's mind, he met the "Holy Ghost" that night. That was the most likely explanation he had at the time for what he felt and saw.

I did not know about his experience with the orbs until many years later. As adults we were swapping spooky stories and found out that- hey, you saw them, too!

VISIONS OF THE LITTLE COUSIN

It was a tragic accident with a loaded gun.

I WAS DATING A GHOST INVESTIGATOR. He was a part-time hobby enthusiast, but he had tools and knowledge and just loved the idea of finding proof! He enjoyed taking EMF readings in houses and cemeteries. He also enjoyed hearing my stories, but he grew a little frightened after what happened in the cemetery with me. That time, it hit a little too close to his heart.

I had already frightened him once before. It was a weekend, and he was spending the night at my place. I woke in the middle of the night to see a tiny lady bending over the bed right beside him. You know how when it is really dark in your room at night, then everything looks gray? This little lady was all grey. Her head was covered, like with an old-fashioned bonnet, and she was very short, probably no taller than four feet. She was whispering to him and he seemed to be talking back. But he was still asleep. She disappeared when she looked up and saw that I was awake. Was it a vision or was it a ghost?

I shook him awake and asked him if he had been dreaming. He was not happy to be shaken out of what he thought was a deep sleep. I told him about the little lady that was talking to him. He was a bit frightened and did not want to believe me. But at the same time, as an investigator, he *did* want to believe me.

Because of that incident, he got some recording devices for my place. Over the course of several months, he would set up the recorders to run at night while we were sleeping. We caught the sound of chairs moving, my piano bench moving, and a couple of spirit voices.

The second time I frightened him, he was testing me. Without me knowing it. (Which, by the way, is a crappy thing to do to people.) He was taking me to a cemetery. I have never had a fear of cemeteries or funeral homes or funerals! I find them to be places of peace. Usually. But not this day.

We were visiting a large cemetery that he knew well. Several of his family members were buried there. We went to visit those family graves and he secretly hoped that I might "connect" with a grandparent that had recently passed away. We were in a newer section of the cemetery, but I kept getting psychically pulled to an older section.

I told him we needed to go to the other side just over the little hill and he asked why. I told him that I had no definite idea why, but that I was getting pulled that way. Whenever your intuition and your gut feelings bring urges to you, listen to them. Often, that is information that you will need or that will keep you safe.

It was too far to walk so we drove to the older section and I told him when to stop the car. I got out and started walking. As I did, a curious shift occurred when I crossed the boundary between the sunlight and the shade of a large oak tree.

I had a vision. I had to stop walking and let this vision play out in my mind. It was like watching an old film. It was like a loop or a section from an old movie that replayed several times. It was the weirdest thing, and very tragic.

In the vision, I find myself as an observer in a trailer house. It is decorated in a style from the late 60s or early 70s. I am hovering near the ceiling against a back wall of the living room. From this perspective, I can see the front door to my left. In front of me is the living room. There is an orange sofa with a long coffee table in front of it. The kitchen and a hallway are just beyond the living room.

There is one person in the room with me. He is a toddler, a little boy with light hair. He looks to be around two or three years old. He is dressed only in a diaper, with no shirt, shoes or pants.

He goes to the front door and pounds on it. There are adults out there, probably his parents or family members, and they are arguing. He babbles something to them, then turns around and wanders back into the living room.

On the long, thin table, there is a coffee cup, a cigarette still smoldering in an ashtray, and a gun. There is no one in the home to stop the toddler from playing with those items. He reaches for the gun. It falls to the floor. At that moment, all I hear is a loud noise and the sound of people yelling.

Then the loop starts all over again: the ceiling, the living room, the kitchen, the child, the noise, the yelling. The loop played in my mind several times, with each loop being about 7-8 seconds long.

Then the vision was over. I blinked, and found myself standing again in the shade of that huge tree. To my partner, it looked like I had been standing there in quiet contemplation for a minute or two.

He walked up behind me and gently called my name. When I turned around my face was pale and streaked with tears. I did not even know I had been crying. But it was soon his turn to cry.

The old section we were in was a final resting place he had forgotten about. He had a young cousin die many years ago from an accidental gunshot. He had never known the little boy and had forgotten that the child was buried in that cemetery. It had been decades ago. I had been pulled there to witness a vision of a child's tragic passing and to connect my partner to his family's past. He never tested me again.

WORKIN' IN THE COAL MINE

What was he looking for?

I WAS WORKING MY SHIFT AT THE RADIO STATION LATE ONE NIGHT. It was the weekend. My shift was 6pm to midnight, on Saturday and Sunday. I loved those weekend shifts. The hustle and bustle of clients and management was gone; it was just me, the music, and the listeners!

A weekend shift meant that you had more flexibility in music choice. I had to stay within the genre of the station (Top 40 country) but if I wanted to pull up some OLD country, say some Johnny Cash, well there was no one to stop me!

At the top of the hour, I had the national and local news feed to broadcast and the local weather forecast to read. About 20 after the hour and then 20 minutes before the hour, I had commercials that broke the flow of the music. But after that it was back to Cash!

The station had been recently remodeled. There were several huge glass windows across the front of the building. Visitors had to walk all the way past that bank of windows to reach the front door. On the weekend shifts I kept the front door locked. There was a doorbell in case someone came to visit me or deliver pizza!

The sound booth, where all the broadcast action happened, was at the back of the building. It had glass windows, too. While I was live on-air, I could still see the front window so I could know if anyone walked up to the front door. I could also see into the production room where we made commercials, and into the breakroom where we could step out the back door and have a smoke break. (I do not smoke; but hey, if smokers get a break, then I should too!)

It was after 10pm, an hour and a half or so before the overnight radio announcer came in to spin records from midnight to 6am. I was in the middle of a commercial break. I caught a glimpse of movement at the front of the building. Some guy was walking up the sidewalk and headed to the front door. And he looked weird. No way I was opening the door. Unless he had pizza.

I finished the break and got the music started back up. Then I realized that no one rang the doorbell. Maybe he changed his mind? I walked out onto the main floor and looked out the front windows. No one was there. Huh? Weird, but whatever.

As I thought about it, I wondered what he had been wearing? It had looked like some weird hat, possibly with a flashlight on top? I guess it is smart to have a light on your hat if you are walking around in the dark at night.

I was back on the air just finishing up another round of commercials when I saw the same man - IN THE BUILDING! It looked like he walked in from the back door and across the break room towards the hallway with the bathrooms. I got a good look then, and realized that he DID have a hat with a lamp on it. And he was wearing dark, dirty pants and a rusty colored shirt. He looked dirty for sure. I also quickly came to the realization that it looked like he was gliding and not walking.

Okay, that was weird. And how did he get in my building? I always make sure both doors are locked before I start a shift. I got back to the music and quietly crept out of the sound booth. I found a baseball bat in the sound booth and reminded myself to ask Randy about that when he came in for his shift.

I walked around the inside of the station with my baseball bat held at the ready, checking doors and rooms. Absolutely no one was there except me.

When the adrenaline wore off, I thought about how strange the man looked. It was as if he was still wearing his work clothes. I think most people would go shower and change out of their grubby work clothes before going out in public. Wherever he worked, it must be a dirty environment. And what was with the hat?

It was nearing midnight and time for Randy to take over. He had showed up about ten minutes prior so he could get prepped for his shift. I asked him if he had ever seen weird things or people in the building. He told me to stick around and we could chat after the news at the top of the hour.

Randy told me a story about coal miners who had died just up the road from our radio station. In the 1920's and 30's there were quite a few mines in the area. Coal mining had started in the region sometime in the late 1800s. This was before Oklahoma was even a state. Most of the mines were shafts dug straight down into the ground. Then they would start digging horizontally from the bottom of the shaft to find coal. It was a dirty and dangerous job. Men died in the mines from explosions, fires, and asphyxiation.

Randy told me to drive up the road about 100 feet. He cautioned that I might want to do it in the daylight instead of midnight. He told me to look for the memorial plaque for the huge explosion that had occurred right below our feet. It was known as the Bolen Mine Disaster.

On Tuesday, December 17th, 1929, at 10:30am, the mine exploded. Seventy men were scheduled for that day's shift. Two out of the seventy had not yet entered the mine when it exploded. Three miners were found alive.

Sixty-one bodies were recovered during the rescue mission. Four men were never found.

Many of the miners were immigrants, mostly Mexican, but Irish and Italian workers were also among the dead. These men came to our country dreaming of a better life, but their dreams were cut short by the need for coal. The Mass Grave of the Mexican Miners in Mount Calvary Cemetery, located in Pittsburg County, Oklahoma, is on the National Register of Historic Places.

So which man came to visit me? Did he know he was dead? Or was he just getting ready for his daily shift and had no idea what was about to happen?

Whenever I go back to visit family or friends, mainly for funerals now, I try to go by that same memorial plaque. I try to take a moment and honor those men who just wanted a better life in this country, but instead entered a different plane of existence.

The radio station is no longer used and has fallen into disrepair. Does a haunting still happen when there is no one to hear or see it? Or maybe the balladeers get together inside and play old songs from their country. With no living persons to interrupt them, the music can just play on and on.

FROM THE MOUTHS OF BABES

Children do not know that ghosts are not "real."

HERE ARE TWO GREAT STORIES FOR YOU THAT COME FROM TWO ADORABLE CHILDREN. The first one is from my son when he was a little over a year old. The next comes from my girlfriend Abby and her daughter, who was about three years old at the time.

My son was born with an immune disorder. He was very sick as a child and still is as an adult. His disorder is more manageable now as he has gotten older and the science of immunology has improved. His first decade of life was full of hospitals and medicines and near-death experiences that innocent children (and their parents) should not go through.

During his first year of life, on one of our stays in the pediatric wing of the ICU, the hospital administrators came to prepare me for my little son's death. That is not what a new mommy needs to hear. I realized it was a possibility and threw myself into learning everything I could about my son's medical condition.

He needed a lot of medicine and a lot of care. It was a tough life, with very little hope. But I vowed to give my all to this little guy.

I had a desire for him to live. But it was not just me. He had some supernatural help in the first years of his little life. And I got to hear about it from the tiny baby, himself.

For some reason, he talked early. Before he was a year old, he could put full sentences together. He was not quoting Shakespeare or anything, but he could talk before he could walk.

He babbled on and on and on. Often, like any exhausted mom, I tuned him out. Especially if we were sitting in the rocking chair, having just finished a book and just about ready for him to go to bed.

Those evenings right before bed were the most peaceful part of the day. Sitting in your mommy's lap, all cuddled up, is comforting to even the sickest child. There were many evenings that we spent more time in the rocking chair than we did anywhere else.

Over the course of several weeks I noticed that he would babble on and seemed to be having a conversation with someone else besides me! There was no one else in the house; my husband had left us, I was a single mom, and he was my only child.

As I paid attention and listened more, I noticed that he was definitely having a conversation with someone or something. And it seemed to be above us, possibly up near the ceiling. He would look up and laugh and babble something to it. I listened closely but could not make out the words he was saying. It was like a separate language just between them.

I watched him closely. And I listened intently. He could definitely hear and see something that I could NOT hear or see.

So how do you ask a tiny baby who is verbal, but still a baby, about something that you cannot see and cannot hear? Ponder that for a while. I did.

Finally, I watched him and saw that he would look at and wave his chubby baby hands to whatever it was. That is how I knew that the activity was happening right at that moment.

And it turns out there was more than one of whatever it was visiting my baby. There was a whole group of them. Angels? Possibly. Cherubs? Maybe. You tell me!

What did my tiny baby tell me was up there? I finally decided to just ask him who he was waving to. His answer startled me. He told me it was "my babies." He had babies? And sure enough, at times that little chubby baby fist would wave hello to more than one entity. There were invisible (to me) "babies" flying around our living room, hanging out above our rocking chair, interacting with my infant.

I asked him what his babies were doing. "Babies help," he told me. Who were they there to help? He pointed to himself and said, "babies help." He pointed to me and said, "babies help Mama."

My infant had angels watching over him. And they were watching over me, too! Just how many "baby" angels I had in my house I will never know. I could not see them. And my baby could not yet count!

I knew then, just like I know now, that there is far more to life and death than we can comprehend. Small children are untouched by the preconceived notions of what is right or wrong, or of what is possible, impossible or fantasy. They experience what they experience without judgment and with total acceptance. Truth comes out of the mouths of our little ones. And wisdom. If we would only listen.

That is why my friend Abby believes the story her little daughter told her about the flying Jesus. This story also involves a sick child. This child though, does not survive.

Through their church, Abby and her girls got to know many other families. One family was struggling with a cancer diagnosis. Their little girl, Emily, was just a year older than Abby's girls.

Little Emily became too sick to go to daycare or church, but the family would update everyone about the progress that she was making. There were some good days when they thought she would make it, but there were not many of them.

Abby's girls would ask about Emily and would include her in their bedtime prayers. It had been several weeks without much good news and her youngest child asked one night if

Emily was going to die. And she wanted to know what did that really mean? What did it mean to die?

It was bedtime and Abby told her girls to climb in bed and they would talk about it in the morning. She secretly hoped they would forget. They did not forget.

Abby's husband worked at the church and had to be there early every morning. She also worked at the church in the daycare. That next morning, she got the girls in the van and they started on the way to the daycare.

As they are driving down the road, the little one speaks up from her car seat in the back, and says, "Mommy, Emily is flying with

Jesus." Abby is startled and asks her to say that one more time. And she says again, "Emily is flying with Jesus."

The little girl goes on to say, "Mommy, I think Emily is flying to heaven. Does this mean she died?"

Abby asks her little girl where she got this idea of flying. The little girl points out the window of their moving vehicle and says, "They are right there, Mommy. They are right there beside us. Emily is flying with Jesus."

Well Abby assured her daughters that everything was fine and that they would check on Emily once they got to the church. She got the girls settled into their day care routine and then hurried off to find her husband.

At the same time, he was coming around the corner to find her. She could tell just by the look on his face. Little Emily had died in the night. The family had just put a call in to the church office to share the news. But Abby already knew. She had already been told that Emily was "flying with Jesus."

DUSTY COMES FOR A VISIT

What a happy little guy!

MY FRIEND, JIM, IS AN ANIMAL LOVER. And animals love him right back! The neighborhood dog with the meanest reputation will scamper around like a puppy and beg for tummy rubs when Jim is around.

Stray dogs routinely show up at his back door, and every one of them gets love along with food and vet care.

When I asked him why he does all that work for stray animals, he told me that animals are kinder and more loving that many people. They have honest and good souls. They are more human than the humans.

The question of the existence of the soul is a difficult one for humans to answer. In a completely non-scientific poll, I asked all the Millennials that I know whether they believe in the soul. They reported that among their peers, there seems to be a trend downward in the belief in a traditional god as defined by traditional religion. But the belief in a soul that exists after death? That idea is still strongly held among their peers.

When I asked specifically about animals having souls, the answer was a resounding yes. And interestingly enough, I had a few young people tell me that they believe all animals have souls but humans who choose to do evil are soulless.

If you ask animal lovers the soul questions, animal lovers like my friend Jim, then you will get a similar answer. Not only do animals have personality, but they also have souls. That is why I was not surprised when he told me about his experience with Dusty.

Jim had gone to visit a friend and his wife. It was one of those old friendships that can pick up right where it left off, even if it had been years since they had seen each other. They stayed up late into the night just talking. There was a lot to catch up on. After a few drinks, and quite a few yawns, they all decided it was time to head to bed.

The master bedroom was downstairs. Jim's guest room was upstairs. He got ready for bed but could not find his phone. After a long search, he remembered that he had last used it in the kitchen.

He headed downstairs and quietly grabbed his phone, trying not to disturb anyone. As he was just about to head back up to his room, he glanced up and saw the cutest little dachshund - also known as a wiener dog - at the top of the stairs.

The little guy was tan all over with long hair and a little beard! His tail was wagging, his eyes were sparkling, and Jim swears the little guy was smiling at him. When Jim got to the top of the stairs, the little doggie was gone. There were two bedrooms at the top of the stairs with a shared bathroom between them. Jim quietly called out for the little dog and searched the rooms. Eventually, he figured the shy pup must have gone back downstairs to be with his owners.

He settled down to sleep, but sometime in the middle of the night, the little guy was back! Jim was in a deep sleep, but he woke up when he heard the doggie at the side of the bed. It was pitch dark in the room, but Jim could hear the long-feathered tail wagging back and forth. He could just imagine a happy grin as the doggie panted hello. The little guy was just begging to come up on the bed for snuggles.

"Okay, mister doggie, you can come on up." Jim heard and felt the little guy scramble up onto the bed. The furry visitor promptly settled down at Jim's feet for a nap. Both of them headed back to sleep.

The next morning the dog was gone again. Jim could smell bacon frying in the kitchen and figured the dog could, too. He headed downstairs, promptly forgetting the encounter as his stomach rumbled when he smelled biscuits to go along with the bacon.

After a hearty breakfast, he asked his friends about the dog.

"So, who was that cute little guy on the stairs last night. I didn't know you guys had a dog! I love dogs," he smiled as he swallowed the last of his coffee.

His friends looked at each other with a strange look.

"Ah, Jim, we don't have one. Are you sure you saw a dog?"

"Yep, it was a dog. Light brown, long hair, even had a beard. Not only did I see it, but it hopped up on my bed in the middle of the night and kept my feet warm."

Jim described the encounter in more detail and his friends sat down in amazement. They told him that it had to be Dusty.

Jim's friend inherited the house when his grandmother died about five years ago. She had lived alone in the house, but was not lonely. For the last fifteen years of her life, a long-haired, bearded wiener dog had been her constant companion. His name was Dusty because with his long hair, Grandma joked that she should use him as a dust mop.

Dusty and Grandma had gone everywhere together, including the salon on Saturdays when she got her hair done. Even to the grocery store. Even the tellers at the bank loved Dusty. No one in the small town minded Dusty's visitations to their business. Grandma knew everyone, and everyone loved her. And Dusty? He loved every person he ever met. He was one of those small dogs with a big personality.

Grandma died five years ago, and Dusty followed quickly after. He lost a little of his sparkle when Grandma died. Just like

Grandma, he lived his whole life in the house and died there, too.

"Well, Jim," his friend asked, "does it freak you out a little about seeing Dusty? Cause I'm a little freaked out myself!"

"Nah," says Jim, "I love dogs. Even ghost ones, I guess. Never met a ghost dog before. Wonder if they have ghost fleas?"

They all laughed and had another cup of coffee!

I am not at all surprised that Jim saw Dusty. Jim loves every animal he meets, especially dogs. If there are ghost dogs, well, Jim would be the perfect person for them to visit.

So, going back to the question of whether animals have souls. If you asked Jim before his encounter with Dusty, he would have said, "probably." Now when you ask if animals have souls, Jim will say, "Absolutely!" He will also tell you that animals are kinder and more loving than humans. They have honest and good souls, and sometimes, dogs are more human than the humans.

CHARLIE SAVES US

Things went bump in the night.

CHARLIE WAS MARRIED TO MY FIRST HUSBAND'S AUNT BESSIE. When I got a divorce, they decided I was family and they wanted to keep me. Of course, I also had an adorable little boy that Bessie loved with all her heart. Charlie and Bessie would feed chips and salsa to my son and ply him with bacon.

They are responsible for the bacon addiction he struggles with to this day.

When I first met Charlie, he was in poor health. His mind and spirit were still sharp and strong, even as his body was failing. He passed away when my little boy was around five years old.

Charlie was about as wide as he was tall. He was a roly-poly, Sicilian man, who loved cigars and smart broads. He once told me I was a smartass and he really liked that. I took it as the highest of compliments.

When Charlie passed away, we knew that Heaven had a new godfather! And we had a new guardian angel, although he probably needed some really large wings. We had no idea how true that image of Charlie as our guardian angel would become.

My little son and I lived in a small apartment complex that was in the middle of an apartment village. As a single mom, finances were tight. I could not afford to buy a home for us, so we lived in the best apartment I could get. Apartment complexes naturally have a fluid group of residents. It is not the most stable living environment. And there tends to be a higher amount of crime associated with apartment complexes.

The summer after Charlie died, there was a sexual predator in the area. He was targeting both children and adult women. My son and I lived on the lower level of the complex, and towards the back where traffic could enter and exit through an access road without much notice. We were in a prime target area that this predator had already scoped out.

Just a few doors down from us, a child had been assaulted in the night. This evil man had broken into her bedroom, slicing the screen off and entering through the window. An adult woman had been assaulted earlier that month in the building next to ours. Everyone in the area was on edge. Even with increased police patrols, the neighborhood was frightened. We kept a closer watch on each other and our children during that time.

One evening, my brother came over to babysit so I could go out. I spent the evening with Charlie and Bessie's daughter. We had gone out for dinner at one of his favorite places. It was close to his birthday. We talked all evening about him and their home life, and how he and Bessie were opposites and yet built a life together. We just laughed and told lots of stories all evening long.

As we were leaving, she told me to be careful. She told me that Charlie had loved me so much, and that if it was possible, he would be watching out for me and my son. Neither of us had any idea that night how important his love from beyond the grave would be. Because that night, we got evidence that my son and I were the target of that predator.

As I was headed back home, where my brother was probably letting my son stay up way too late, I was thinking about Charlie and how witty he had been. And how fierce! People made the mistake of thinking he was a short, fat man with no muscles and no strength. They only made that mistake once.

Charlie had been tough and solid. And he would do anything to protect his family. His favorite weapon was a tire iron. If someone threatened his girls, or his property, they were on his list.   Trespassers on his private property had been known to meet Charlie and need work on their knees after that "meeting."

After I got home, I thanked my brother and got my kiddo back into bed. We stayed up talking quietly until my son was finally asleep. My brother was worried about the stories he had seen on the news. He knew our apartment complex was dangerous. I told him not to worry because I kept the phone nearby, and I would call him if anything concerned me!

When my brother left, I got ready for bed. I double checked all the locks and turned off my cell phone alarm. It was the weekend, and I planned to sleep-in the next morning, unless my son woke me up for cartoons and pancakes.

In the middle of the night, my son's alarm clock started going off. It was around 2:30am. I was so angry. I stormed into his room where he gave me that sleepy "I don't know" look. He said that he did not set an alarm, and I certainly did not set one in his room. We checked the clock and made sure there was no alarm set. Very weird.

I got him settled back down and I had just drifted back to sleep when another alarm went off! This time it was the clock in my room. I know I had definitely NOT set that alarm. It had just been ten minutes since my son's alarm went off.

Okay, what was happening?   This time my son came bouncing into my room accusing ME of setting an alarm.   He thought it was great fun. He had turned the hall light on, and the light was on in my bedroom. Within just a few minutes the alarm goes off in his room again! We rushed in and turned his bedroom light on.

Then, while we were standing in his room and laughing - because at that point all we could do was laugh - the alarm goes off one more time in my bedroom!   By this time, we were fully awake.   All the lights were on in the house. We were making plenty of noise. I decided at this point it would be even harder to get my excited 5-year old back to bed, so we chose to go into the kitchen and make cocoa instead.

We were laughing about the night's adventure and sipping our soy cocoa, when my son asked me if I could smell the cigar, "Hey mom, that's smells just like Uncle Charlie." Well, I nearly dropped my cocoa!

We tried to figure out what had just happened. My son had unfortunately seen the news report about someone hurting the little girl just a few doors down from us. With the wisdom of children, he told me, "Well, maybe

Uncle Charlie set those alarms for us. Maybe that bad guy was in the neighborhood and he wanted us to be safe."

I nearly dropped my cocoa again. My goodness. Could he be right? It would have been obvious to anyone standing outside that we were wide awake and actively aware. Every light was on in our apartment and we were making enough noise that I am surprised we did not wake up our neighbors. If predator's look for easy prey, then they would have definitely skipped us. A predator would have been stupid to pick us.

Eventually, I got my son back in bed. Tucked in safely, he quickly went back to sleep. My brother was a night owl, so I knew he would be awake. I texted him and told him what had happened. He agreed that it was supremely weird. He also agreed to come over the next day to look around, and to bring over some heavy-duty locks for our windows. I did not get much sleep the rest of that night.

The next day my brother and I quickly reached a frightening conclusion. We think someone really was standing outside my son's room that night. The screen to his bedroom window had been removed. It looked like someone had tried to cut the screen out at first, and then just pulled the whole screen frame off the window. The bent frame was lying on the ground right under my son's window, hidden behind a bush.

My son and I still talk about the night Charlie scared off the bad guy. And no tire iron was needed. Just a roly-poly angel with a cigar. It just goes to show you that guardian angels may come in various shapes and sizes, but all of them are motivated by love.

HUGGED BY AN ANGEL

It was a bit of love from the beyond.

MY FRIEND MINNIE SURPRISED ME ONE DAY WITH THIS TOUCHING TALE. She is best friends with my deceased husband's mother, Jen. (I will tell you a great story about my last husband, David, in the last chapter.)

Minnie and Jen had come to town to have lunch with me. As usual, they asked how my new hubby was doing. It is always amazing to me that love will grow anywhere that you let it in. My new hubby and my old mother-in-law were connected by their love for me. Jen did not have a son anymore, and my new hubby's parents were deceased, so they decided they would be family to each other!

During lunch, we talked about our love lives, and you would be surprised at how much little old ladies love little old men. Their slightly naughty stories shocked me, which they thought was great fun.

For some reason we started talking about ghosts. We were talking about love, and how love does not end even when life does. I told them my story about David returning to check on me. They loved it! And then Minnie told me her story of love from the great beyond.

Decades ago, she was a young mother with two little children. Her baby daughter was just nine months old. Her husband was a hard-working man who adored his wife and kids. He worked a job as an electrical foreman. He ran lines and managed electrical stations in rural areas of our country as access to electricity spread throughout America. Most people do not realize that parts of rural

America did not have electricity until the 1950s. It was a dangerous job, but he was good at it. And it paid well.

It was already late when he got a call to come back to a local work site. Something had broken down and he was needed. The kids were already in bed, so he hugged Minnie bye and said that he would be back quickly because it was a simple fix.

Hours later, she was wild with worry. There were no cell phones to call or text, businesses were all shut down, and she could not leave her children alone in the house while she went looking for information. She did not know what to do, but had a troubling feeling that something bad was happening.

She remembered one of her friends that was a night worker at city hall dispatch. She called her friend to ask if there had been any news about car wrecks or accidents at her husband's work site.

He told her, "Minnie, I have not heard anything, but let me put you on hold and see what I can find out." As she was standing there, holding the phone to her ear and waiting for news, she became more and more frightened.

The minutes ticked by on the kitchen clock, and then in the quiet she heard something very unexpected in her little country house. She heard what sounded like enormous wings beating above her! She felt a cool breeze, but before she could even look up to see what was happening, strong arms wrapped around her from behind.

She was so startled that she nearly dropped the phone. She could not SEE anything, but she could sure FEEL it. It felt like total warmth and comfort and love. While she was held in those invisible arms, all her worry was taken away. There was no more fear, no more anguish. She felt totally at peace. She relaxed into those arms and knew she was being held by something sent to give her comfort and strength. And she needed it.

Those strong arms held her as her friend came back onto the line, "Minnie, there's been an accident. Can you find someone to watch the kids? Are they asleep? I'm going to send a police cruiser over to get you. Minnie, it's not good. I'm so sorry."

Her legs gave out as she realized in that instant that her husband was dead. But she did not fall! She was held upright in the arms of this invisible winged visitor.

She breathed deeply and hung up the phone. As she felt her steadiness grow, the wings slowly released her. She was standing on her own two feet again. She felt the cool breeze, and then the angelic visitor was gone in the blink of an eye!

She found the strength to make it through that tragic time. Her little girl had just started speaking and the first word she said was "dada." Even though he was gone, Minnie still felt his presence. Throughout the years, she told the children about their dad and never let them forget him.

The angel? She never felt the cool breeze and the loving arms again. It was a once-in-a-lifetime experience. There have been plenty of other tragedies in her life. But she says that single experience of being held in the loving arms of an angel was enough to give her a lifetime of comfort and strength.

As she looks back on that day, she likes to think that maybe it was her husband. When she finally got the news from her friend in dispatch, her husband was already dead. Was he coming to give her one last hug? Maybe he had already gotten his angelic wings! Whoever the visitor was, Minnie is convinced that love exists beyond death.

THE 3 KNOCKS

When everyone else finally hears it, too.

HERE IS THE OTHER SPOOKY STORY I PROMISED TO TELL YOU ABOUT MY CHILDHOOD HOME. One of the most frustrating things about investigating ghosts, angels, bigfoot, the Loch Ness monster, UFOs, Yeti, demons, or any other supernatural phenomena, is when you are alone and no one else can verify the story. It is easy to discount someone and say, "well, they were all alone and probably hysterical." But when other people have the same experience? Ah, that is priceless proof.

It was the summer of 1983. I had just graduated from high school. My oldest sister was visiting at home for the summer. She was leaving soon to work on her doctorate. She had just finished up with her bachelor's degree and had been away at college for several years. The oldest daughter living at home got to have the "premium" child's bedroom at the left, front corner of the house. That was my room, but not for much longer. I would be moving out at the end of the summer to go to college, so my little sister would get to have the "big girl's" room. It was a big deal.

Our house was long, sort of like a stretched-out ranch home in the layout. When you saw the house from the front, from left to right, there were two bedrooms, the front door, the dining room with a large bay window, the kitchen and then the family room/garage on the end. On the back side, there were two more bedrooms, two bathrooms, the living room, and then the family room at the end. It was a big house on the prairie. (You need to understand the layout of the house when you hear what happened!)

That summer I spent like I did most summers: reading! I was a pale, book-loving child, who has turned into a pale, book-loving adult. The summer sun was way too hot for me and it just kicked up my allergies, anyway. I read all day long. And into the night, too.

The first time I heard the knockings, it was early in the summer. It was late in the night, well past midnight. Mom caught me up late reading in bed and took away my flashlight! But I had an alternate plan. I would lay on the floor and turn on the closet light. My closet door was louvered, so there was just enough light coming through the slats to illuminate my book.

I knew I had to take a break when I kept falling asleep and needed to read a passage more than once. Okay, it was time to actually go to bed. I turned out the light and quietly slipped into bed.

Now, a little note about living in the deep rural country. People who live in cities just cannot really understand this, but it is DARK! I mean, it is so dark out in the boonies, that at certain times of the moon phases, you can barely see your hand in front of you.

We did not have close neighbors. So, there were no extra lights from their houses. And we did not have a pole light, which is a large light that the electric co-op will put up in your yard, especially if you have a barn near the house. Our barn was over on the other 60 acres. We did have a flood light on the corner of the house. There was a switch in my parents' bedroom, but that light was not often used. It was only for "emergencies."

Now, with the lack of neighbors, we also did not have a huge need for privacy curtains. Sure, we had curtains, but they were more like filmy, flimsy, gossamer things that were mainly for decoration. Many of the windows had roll-up pull shades that were almost always rolled up.

When I crawled into bed that night, the bedroom and closet doors were to the right.

There was a window to the foot of my bed. The window to the left of my bed was the end window on the front side of the house. I was exhausted and just about asleep when I heard a strange noise:

Knock, knock, knock.

Knock, knock, knock.

Knock, knock, knock.

There was a slight pause, and then it started up again.

Knock, knock, knock.

Knock, knock, knock.

Knock, knock, knock.

Something was knocking at my window. I ignored it. Okay, I was really sleepy, and part of me thought I was just imagining it. I had been reading some scary and weird books, and I have a great imagination. It was easy for me to dismiss it as just "the wind."

I promptly forgot about it. Until it happened again, about two weeks later. The exact same scenario occurred, just with a different book. Late night, very dark outside, shades up, flimsy curtains down, I turn off the closet light and climb into bed. Just as I was drifting off to sleep, I heard it again. This time I paid attention.

Knock, knock, knock.

Knock, knock, knock.

Knock, knock, knock.

Knock, knock, knock.

Knock, knock, knock.

Knock, knock, knock.

Knock, knock, knock.

Knock, knock, knock.

Knock, knock, knock.

It was a series of three knocks repeated in quick succession three times. Then there was a slight pause, and the three knocks were repeated three more times. Another slight pause, and once again, the series of three knocks repeated three times.

Okay, that was freaky. It wasn't a loud knocking. It wasn't banging on the window. It was just a friendly knocking from something or someone? Maybe some ugly swamp monster? In the middle of the dark night? What the heck?

Now, please remember that I wear glasses. Remember the story about the balls of light? Everything is fuzzy when I take off my glasses. And it was deep country dark outside. I did not want to move or turn my head to try to see what might be outside my window. If I could see "IT" then it could see me, too. I felt like an animal at the zoo just trying to catch a nap and someone was rapping at my cage.

So, that second time, I just lay there. I was frightened and breathing hard. I listened for movement. I listened for the crackle of sticks and leaves breaking under footsteps. Of course, this would have been hard to hear, since the windows were closed, and the air-cooler was running full blast. It was summer, after all.

While lying there, waiting for sounds or more knocks, I was really thankful it was summer and the windows were closed! If the windows had been open to let in a cool, night-time breeze, then maybe Bigfoot would have taken off with his new, very pale, nearsighted bride. I wondered if he would have given me a chance to grab my glasses?

I realized at that point, with that train of thought, that I might be a bit hysterical. There had been no more knockings since that original set of 3X3X3. I calmed myself down, and decided it was safe to move and look out the window. There was absolutely nothing there.

The next time it happened, I vowed to be prepared to look out the window the first chance I got. I started going to bed with my glasses ON! It was about another week when it happened again. This time, I had just fallen asleep when the knockings started up. I slowly and quietly rolled over to see what was at the window. Nothing was there. Absolutely nothing.

I could still hear the knocks. There was no shadowy presence, no wispy presence, no presence at all. What was going on? I had enough courage to slowly crawl out of bed and over to the window. By this time, the knocks had stopped. Nothing. There was nothing there. I heard it one more time that summer in that corner bedroom, and the pattern was always the same series of knocks.

Eventually, it was time for me to give up my corner bedroom. My little sister would be the last girl at home. I was packing up most things to move into my new dorm room. Whatever I left behind would be moved into the middle bedroom that I would share with my older sister when she also came back from college to visit.

My little sister finally got all her things moved into the corner bedroom. It was late in the summer. She and I had been up late chatting. The door to Mom and Dad's room, just across the hallway, was closed. Our bedroom doors were open so we could chat until we drifted off to sleep.

I heard her sit up in bed. She said, "Shanna, did you just knock on the wall?" I told her that it wasn't me. "Well, something is knocking on my window." I told her to meet me in the hallway!

I quickly updated her on what had been going on. She was upset that I had been hearing it all summer long and had told no one. She decided that we needed to tell Mom and Dad. We knocked on their door and woke them both up. My little sister told them what she had just heard, and then I told them that I had been hearing it all summer long.

Dad was a pragmatic fellow. He asked if we had turned on the flood light. Well, no. "Okay, then, turn it on," he said. "Now go look and see if there's anything out there."

So that's what we did. There was nothing there. I already knew that we would see nothing. But Dad told us to go back to bed. If nothing was there, then nothing was there.

"But Dad, what is making all those knocks?" little sister asked. He responded that it was just the wind, or a bird or a tree limb. Yeah, right. A bird that pecks on the window at night in a series of 3X3X3 knocks? Nope, I did not buy that, and neither did my little sister.

We were laughed at that next morning. Dad made sure to remind us that our entire property was fenced, and the house had a chain-link fence around it with locking gates. And on top of that, we had dogs, hunting dogs that lived outside and never once sounded the alarm that "something" or "someone" was there. Dad said it was just our imaginations.

Our oldest sister was home visiting for the weekend. She made fun of us, too. She was the rational scientist, she said, and we were just hysterical girls. Well, she became a bit hysterical later that night.

She and I were in the middle bedroom; little sister was in the corner room. Older sis was in a twin bed that was against the outer wall, right next to a window that faced the front of the house. Mom and Dad were asleep, and we girls had just all gone to bed.

I was nearly asleep when my older sister sat bolt upright in bed and said, "I hear knocking! Something is knocking on the kitchen window."

Sure enough, we grabbed our little sister and stood in the hallway. We all listened in amazement. But this time, it was different. It was still a series of three knocks – knock, knock, knock. But this time it was much faster. It was knocking on all the windows across the front of the house in rapid succession.

"Knock, knock, knock" on the kitchen window.

"Knock, knock, knock" on the dining room bay window.

"Knock, knock, knock" on the middle bedroom window.

"Knock, knock, knock" on the corner bedroom window.

And then it started immediately again on the kitchen window without stopping. This time, the knocking was loud. And it was getting louder. We did not take time to wake up our parents. The knocking was loud enough to wake them for us.

"What the heck is this?" my dad asked, to which little sister and I replied, "This is what we were trying to tell you about!"

My mom went to check in on my little brother, who was only about six years old. He had slept through all the other knockings, but this was loud enough to wake everyone up.

As the knocking continued, Dad came up with a plan. We had guns. We were country folks. There was a shotgun behind every door. And we knew how to load and shoot. He stationed each of us girls with a gun at each of the main entries to the house. Big sis was at the sliding glass doors at the back. Little sis was at the family room door. I was at the front door.

Dad was going out there. With a gun. He had one simple rule for me at the front door,

"If you see me running, then let me in. If it's not me, then don't let it in."

We quietly and slowly opened the front door. Dad stepped out onto the front porch. In that instant, the entire phenomenon went quiet. There was no sound. Even the summer crickets went quiet.

My Dad has always been a country boy, and had learned to hunt and track game when he was little. He used all of his skills to try to find the source of the knockings. He searched for footprints. He searched for car tracks. He searched for broken twigs. He searched around the house, checking every door, every window and every lock on the chain-link fences.   Nothing was broken, nothing was disturbed.

He even checked in on his bird dogs. They were snoring away, as if nothing had disturbed their slumber. They woke up drowsily to join in on the rest of his patrol.

Dad checked the roof of the house for access, for footprints, for any indication that someone had been up there. None. He checked the trees that were inside the chain-link fence and those just out of the fenced area for indications of a presence. None.

He checked our parked vehicles to see if anyone had been near them. He even walked partway down our country road in the dark, sat a spell, and turned back to scan our home for any movement.

Nothing. He found nothing. He came back in the house, amazed and confused.

My older sister and I both headed to college just a few weeks later. My younger sister and brother were still living at home, but no one in the family ever heard the knockings again. It remains a family mystery.

Everyone in my family has a different interpretation of that summer. Earlier in the year, my dad caught some kids egging our house one night. He told us that maybe it was just those kids again. I think he was just trying to calm us all down. But none of us believed it.

The knockings were too fast, too loud, and too weird. Also, our dogs would have ripped anyone apart who got that close to the house, and they never once acted like they saw or heard anything.

Me? I am no closer to knowing what it is now than I was back then. I have often thought about going back to investigate that house, but it burned to the ground several years ago.

It happened only during that one summer. And it seemed to occur only when every light was turned off in the house. And it seemed to focus, at least in the beginning, on me or my bedroom.

I am convinced that it must be supernatural, because I do not know of any human, bird, creature, or tree that would knock in a pattern like that. But supernatural what? Bigfoot? Aliens? Ghosts? Your guess is as good as mine.

DAVID RETURNS

A blessing for my new husband.

DAVID WAS ONLY FORTY-SIX YEARS OLD WHEN HE DIED UNEXPECTEDLY. We were newlyweds and had been married just eleven months. I had been a single mom, raising a child on disability for the previous sixteen years. David and I got married when my son turned eighteen.

After the shock of his death, I had to deal with probate, insurance, medical bills from his trip to the emergency room, and all sorts of unexpected surprises that are left for surviving spouses. It was an awful ordeal.

I was lucky in only one way. My son has been very sick all his life. I had become accustomed to the knowledge that he could die at any time. I think people who suffer the most when a loved one dies are the people who are in deep denial. I was not in denial. I had grown accustomed to the possibility of my child's death, so I was able to face my husband's death and learn how to eventually process and let go of much of that pain.

It was hard! Death, especially unexpected death, is hard to wrap your mind around. At first, I tried counseling. I joined a few grief groups for surviving spouses. What I noticed at first was that I was the youngest widow there. Then I noticed that some of the women were still in mourning, even twenty years after their spouse died. I had zero plans for perpetual mourning.

Every person will experience grief in their own way. And any way that you can process the pain is the right way for you. Eventually, I found ways to deal with the loss and move on.

David had been my second husband, so I figured I was done with men. There would be no one else for me. I was too old. I was not interested in relationships. No more dating, love, or sex. I was going to become a hermit poet and live in a forest of peace. But then, I met Mark.

It was an accident that we met. A tiny little bit of kismet. I guess it was truly meant to be. He had also been a single parent, having raised his son all alone after his wife bailed on them. He and I shared similar religious views, important similar personality traits, and he was just the right type of happy-go-lucky man to balance out my dark, brooding Irish nature. Yin and Yang! It was an irresistible pull.

Less than a year after David's death, Mark asked me to marry him. He had waited his whole life to find me, he said, and he did not care what anyone thought.

Well, I was conflicted. What would people say about me? That I was a widow who married too quickly? The people who mattered most to me did not care. They just wanted me to be happy. Mark did not care. He just wanted me.

Mark made it easy, too. He got to know David through me. He got to be friends with my deceased husband. He was never upset when I needed to talk about David or the family issues or how conflicted I was feeling. He just loved me through it all.

What is even more amazing is that David's mother did not have a son anymore, and Mark's parents had already passed away. So, the two of them decided they would love each other like family, because of the love that David and I had shared.

It turns out that David and Mark shared a lot of common traits. They both loved airplanes! David had been a pilot, and Mark's family had a plane that he flew when he was growing up. They both loved the water and boats. They were fans of 80s music; they collected broadcast equipment; both were computer programming nerds; they were fans of science fiction and fantasy; but most importantly, they both adored me.

Mark came to the place where he believed that they would have been best friends if they had been able to meet. I think that is quite possible. If David had chosen someone for me, it could not have been a better man than Mark!

It became easy to settle into my new life with my new partner. David easily became a part of our life together. He was like an unseen family member. Until one night, right before our wedding, when the unseen showed up!

Mark and I have very different schedules. Even though I am not a morning person, I still had to be at work by 8 am. And I needed a full eight hours of sleep. Mark did not go into his office until 10 am each morning, and he needed much less sleep than I did. So, he went to bed later and got up later.

I sleep with a mask on every night. It helps block streetlights and nightlights, and it just helps me have a better quality of sleep. On the weekends, I leave a nightlight on in the bedroom when I go to bed. It is just enough light so that a slightly inebriated Mark can see to get his pajamas on and doesn't have to turn on the overhead light when he comes in the room.

On the weekends, Mark likes to turn the 80s music up really loud. We drink a few beers and play pool. (Did I mention that they both were great pool players?) We have a party for two every weekend at our house.

It was one of those weekends when David showed up. I had gone to bed around midnight. I sleep on the left side of the bed, and I typically sleep curled up on my left side. When Mark crawls into bed on the right side, I have gotten into the habit, even if I am deeply asleep, of reaching out behind me with my right hand to pat him and tell him "goodnight."

So that night, when I felt the bed move like someone had just crawled in, I reached out to pat Mark and say, "goodnight." But Mark was not there. I felt around and no one was there. Well, that woke me up enough to roll over and take off my mask to see what was going on.

When I looked over at Mark's side of the bed, all I saw was a fuzzy figure standing there. I wondered why Mark had climbed into bed and then out again. That was weird.

Something else was wrong. Mark did not say anything. And then I tried to focus and look closer. Someone was there. But maybe it was not Mark? You would think that I would have been terrified at that moment, but I was not. My gut feeling, my intuition, was not telling me to be afraid. At least, not yet!

As I looked closer, the human shape I saw did not seem fully formed. It looked fuzzy. It was grey and see-through. I could see the dresser behind the figure. And it was tall, taller than Mark. When it started moving, that is when I recognized him.

Mark is 6' tall, but David had been 6'4" and well over 300 pounds. It looked like David was in my bedroom. Was he coming to check on me?

I was not scared until he started walking. Or floating. I could not see if he had feet. He "walked" around the bed, from Mark's side, across the floor at the foot of the bed, and then towards me on my side of the bed.

David had certain mannerisms and ways that he moved his head and body. When he looked at me as he crossed the foot of the bed, I shivered. Yes, I could see eyes! It was him! When he started walking toward me on my side of the bed, I sat fully up and held my right arm out with my hand in the "stop" pose.

To the ghost of my dead husband, I said, "Please stop, you are scaring me." Of course, he stopped and just looked at me. I think he smiled, but I wasn't sure. I needed my glasses. I reached back with my left hand to grab them and glanced away for just a moment. That one glance broke the connection. The spirit vanished! David was gone.

There is no telling how much energy it took for him to contact me. He had moved the bed to get my attention, shaped recognizable human form, and had understood my communication. I was amazed and tremendously touched that he had made so much effort to reach out to me.

I think he was coming to give a blessing on my new marriage. At least, that is what I like to think. He did not seem angry or upset, he just seemed like he wanted to see me one last time.

I took a sip of water to calm my slightly frazzled nerves. Okay, should I walk out there and tell Mark? He probably had a few shots of whiskey in him. I felt that whiskey might be just what I needed, too. But no. I decided to save the conversation for brunch the next day, when Mark was sober, and I was a little less shaken.

Although I did text him. "Hey honey, I just saw a ghost. Remind me tomorrow to tell you all about it."

The music played on. Mark was probably making nachos at that moment and did not hear his phone ding. It was okay. We would talk in the morning. That was a conversation best had in the bright daylight over coffee and toast. And maybe a good shot of whiskey!

David has never been seen since that one visit. The little house we had been living in when he passed away is now a rental home. I often wonder if the renters ever see his spirit. But I do not think David is haunting the rental house. Often, hauntings occur when spirits are stuck in a location, and often they do not even realize that they are dead.

David had come to see me one last time, and show me that he still cared. He was not stuck like a ghost in a residual haunting. He was just stopping by to say a final goodbye. I wonder if he will ever come back to visit again. He is probably watching us right now from afar, just waiting for the day when we can be reconnected and he can meet his new best friend, Mark!

FINAL THOUGHTS

"We are such stuff as dreams are made on,
and our little life is rounded with a sleep."
- William Shakespeare

SO, DO YOU BELIEVE? Do you believe now after reading these stories? Here is what I know about people: if you believed before reading this book, you probably still believe;

and if you did *not* believe before reading this book, then you probably still do not.

Most of the time, we keep our beliefs until something shakes that foundation and forces us to rethink what we think! That is how it is with ghosts. Until you see one yourself, until you see incontrovertible evidence that you just cannot deny, then you may never believe. And that is okay.

Many days, I am still not sure that I believe 100% in ghosts. When I start pondering all the things I have seen and experienced, then I know there is more to life and death than what we understand. Of this I am totally convinced – we do not know everything. And this is the distinction I would love for you to come away with after reading my ghost stories – there is far more in our world that is unknown than what is known. We tiny humans, on this tiny whirling ball, in this huge expanding universe, are delusional if we think that we "know" much at all.

So, to all you doubters, and to all you true believers, let me just say that I am right there with you! It just depends on what day of the week you ask me.

My husband loves to point out that I "say" that I am agnostic on the idea of ghosts and an afterlife, but that I am really a true believer. Some days, I am convinced that all there is after this life is a dirt nap. There is nothing else.

That idea is great motivation! When today, this life, this here and now, is ALL you are guaranteed, then you had better enjoy this one life you are given to its full extent.

So, in the end, whether you believe in ghosts or you do not, it does not matter at all. Someday, each and every one of us is going to die. Then, and only then, will each of us find out for sure.

THE END

* * *

BONUS STORY

(Yes, this is a true story, too. But it is a very NON-supernatural story about a spooky and possibly supernatural location. Enjoy!)

MOUNTAIN STATION is a graveyard on what was an old stagecoach route that ran through Oklahoma back in the mid-1800s, way before Oklahoma was a state. Growing up on a farm near that graveyard, and near several others, I was taught to have respect for the deceased and for history. But some kids were not taught that way.

Mountain Station became a hangout for high school kids who wanted to get drunk, or who wanted to search for witches' graves and ghosts. It was kind of a joke. It was out in the middle of nowhere, in a county that is rural to begin with. To get there, you had to take curvy dirt roads that go up to the top of the mountain and down the other side.

There was nothing around except trees, some rocky pasture land, and the dead. Unless you were one of the unlucky kids who got harassed there at Halloween by some unseen, and presumably, evil forces. I know. But it was truly a case of mistaken identity.

Yes, there were stories about people getting caught at Mountain Station late at night and the car would not start. I never experienced that. There were even stories that some people found scratch marks on their trucks after visiting the cemetery. I think that had far more to do with the brushy, unkempt nature of the roads that led up to the cemetery.

But the stories about the creepy chanting noises and the dark hooded figures? Those stories are absolutely true, they are based in fact. I know. I was there, along with one of my friends, who shall remain unnamed.

It was Halloween, which is my absolute favorite holiday. I do not remember the exact year, but the first time we haunted Mountain Station, it was sometime in the early 80s.

Looking back, we are incredibly lucky that no one ever shot at us! Everyone in rural Oklahoma has a gun, and every truck has a gun rack. I think no one shot at us because they were all running as fast and as far away from us as possible.

My dad, bless his mischievous heart, had agreed to take us up near Mountain Station cemetery. My friend and I were wearing black hooded robes. They were just choir robes from a fancy Baptist church. We borrowed them for the night!

When we got close to the cemetery, dad turned off the truck lights so no one would see us coming. We drove that last half mile in the dark. There were quite a few cars in front of the cemetery. It was full of high school kids, drinking and roaming around in the dark, looking for those witches and ghosts.

Dad pointed out where we could walk around to get to the back side of the cemetery.

My co-conspirator and I got into position. No one saw us, at first. They were all too busy drinking and listening to boom boxes. There were a few flashlights and lanterns which only added to the spooky vibe. It was a perfect situation for unseen, and presumably, evil forces.

We were standing about 25 feet apart at the back of the cemetery. Our plan was to start walking forward through the cemetery while chanting something like, "ooomm, aaamm, homina, homina" over and over. We started out walking and chanting, but had to work hard to be heard over the music. With our hooded black robes on, and our hands held out in front of us, I am quite sure we looked exactly as scary as we thought we did.

We stopped about halfway in, and chanted louder. And yes, we cleared out that cemetery. There were actually more people there than we imagined. For some reason, there were drunk kids sitting in the trees. One of them fell from a limb just above my head and nearly landed on me, but they ran off screaming before I could even jump back. I just kept chanting!

A slight level of inebriation kept everyone from breaking their ankles or legs as they ran screaming out of the cemetery. I think they all sobered up pretty quickly! It did not take long for the vehicles to race down the dirt roads and back towards the safety of town, leaving Mountain Station a quiet and peaceful resting place for the dead once again.

Well, except for the laughing. My dad was doubled over, holding on to the side of his truck for support, laughing so hard that he nearly split his overalls.

My buddy and I never told anyone what we had done. For the next several weeks at school, it was all anyone was talking about. There were even new prayer groups started at school because of it. And I am quite sure that some kids gave up drinking all together. When anyone would ask us, we would just shake our heads and agree with all of our friends - yep, something really strange happened up at Mountain Station!

END NOTES – I am available for speaking engagements to discuss hauntings, Bigfoot, UFOs, and all manner of spooky stuff.

Please have an idea of the size of the venue, average attendance, and the dates of the conference or event. For speaker's fees and other information, send me an email at: chatwithshanna@gmail.com

I am NOT available to cleanse your house. A haunting can be a dangerous situation and is not something to play around with. Proceed with caution. Begin first with your local ghost enthusiast groups. You can often find a local group on Facebook or go into the local metaphysical shop and ask around. You might also request a house blessing from your local religious leader.

THE END

(This time, for real!)